# Compass

by Sheila Rivera

first step nonfiction

Lerner Publications Company · Minneapolis

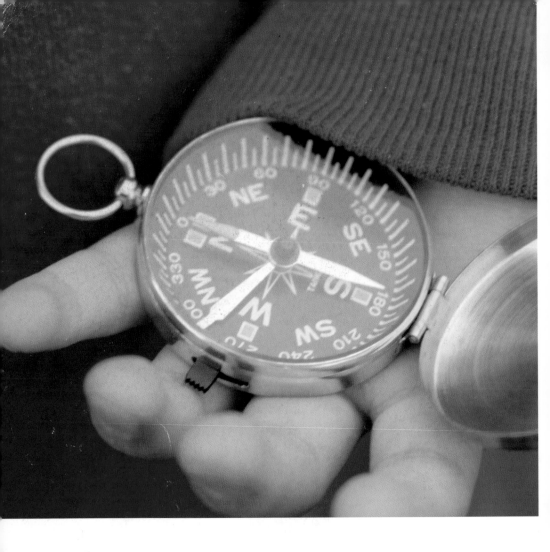

What do you do with
a compass?

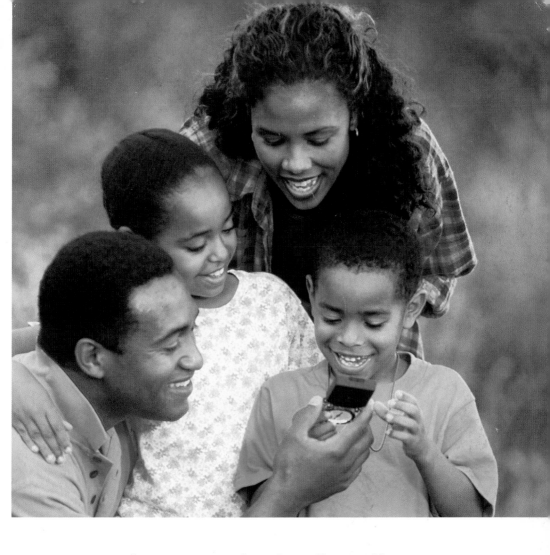

I see what direction
I am looking.

3

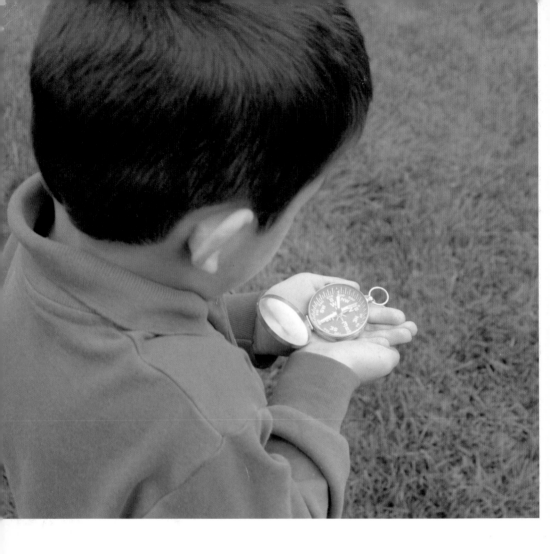

I look north.

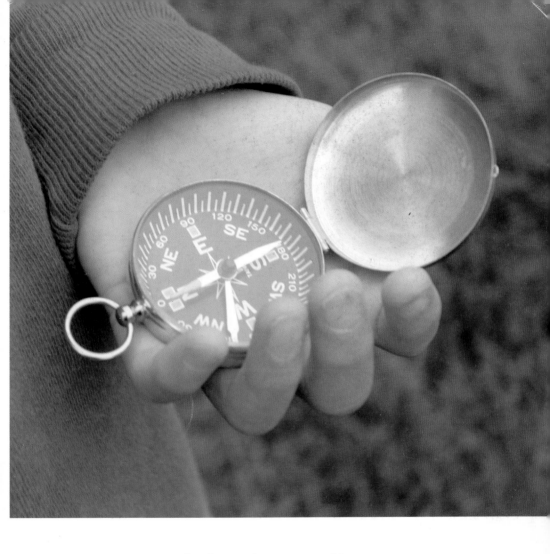

I look south.

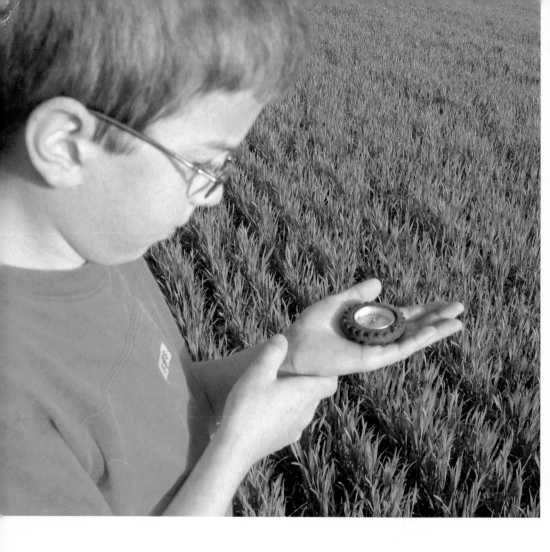

I look east.

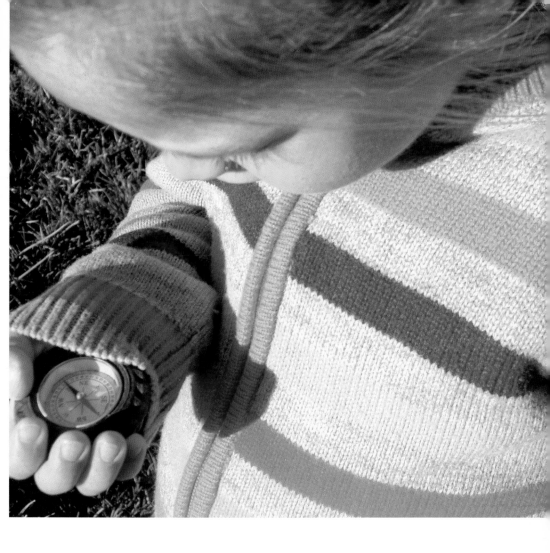

I look west.

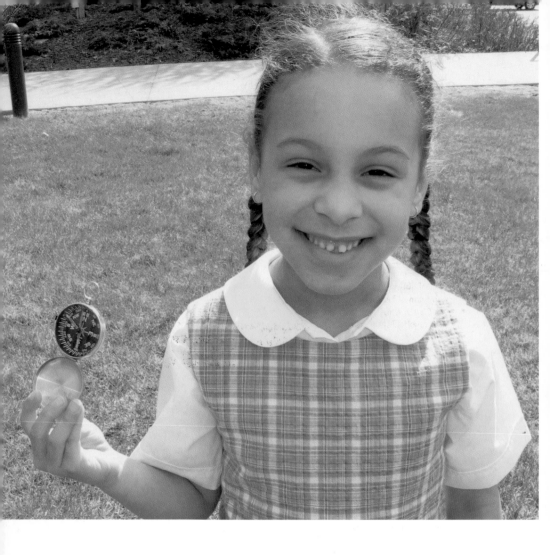

Can you use a compass?